his far. Congratulations and b

bound within these pages wi

magnificent, fantastical world

and situations – and you will never be the same

This is how it starts – with a small taste, a nibble, a glimpse into worl
beyond. This is how it will end – you won't be able to wait for the ne
volume, you'll hunt it down, get it any way you can. In time you'll acquire
new name (Kagome, Saotome, Aya or something similiar), a new set
friends not bound by distance or location—linked by a shared passion. Yo
will become one of us – a VIZionary.

So, who are we? We're VIZ – we started out 17 years ago when 2 fans bor
raised and fed Japanese manga relocated from Japan to San Francisc
California, and decided to share their passion for Japanese manga to th
United States. Okay, so they did try to keep it a secret, but then YOU cam
along, with your fansites, your letters, your petitions, your clubs in eve
state, every city. We couldn't get it fast enough for you.

We couldn't take everyone so we took the best and brightest of you to help
get you your manga. They/We are still among you – on the websites, at t
conventions – everywhere listening to you. We're even owned by two
Japan's largest publishing companies so we can feed your need.

Don't settle for imitation manga – we've been around for much longer th
those other companies that pop up whenever they smell a fad. We've be
bridging the gap between Japan and the US for over 17 years and we kno
the real manga. And so do you. So come on, open up, join us and becom
a VIZionary.

Welcome to the Viz graphic novel sampler, a sneak peek into ? brand-new manga from Viz.

These are some of the most exciting, funniest, romantic, thought-provoking and hottest manga to launch from Japan to North America this Summer!

VIZ MANGA MEANS VIZ QUALITY!

- The best, most appealing, and unique titles!

- English adaptations that seamlessly bridge the gap between Japanese and English to bring out the subtleties of each character and dialogue!

- Artful lettering and sound effects styled to suit the original artwork!

- Glossaries for unretouched sound effects so you don't miss a single detail of the story!

- High-quality reproduction so you don't miss *a single line* of the artist's original artwork!

Go ahead, flip through this book and sample a title or two for FREE...and remember, there's more where these came from!

Manga SneakPeek 2003
CONTENTS

Cover Designer **Dan Ziegler**   Graphic Designer **Judi Roubideaux**   Creative Services Manager **Clay Walsh**   Editor **Eric Searleman**

BOYS OVER FLOWERS
HANA YORI DANGO
Story & Art **Yoko Kamio**
English Adaptation **Gerard Jones**
Translation **JN Productions**
Editor **Ian Robertson**

"HANA-YORI DANGO" ©1992 by Yoko Kamio
First published in Japan in 1992 by SHUEISHA Inc.
English translation rights in the United States of America and Canada arranged by SHUEISHA Inc. through CLOVERWAY, Inc.

BASARA
Story and Art **Yumi Tamura**
English Adaptation **Gerard Jones**
Translation **Lillian Olsen**
Lettering & Touch-Up Art **Bill Schuch**
Editor **P. Duffield**
Supervising Editor **Ian Robertson**
©1991 Yumi Tamura/Shogakukan
First published by Shogakukan, Inc. in Japan as "Basara."

WEDDING PEACH
Created **Sukehiro Tomita**
Story & Art **Nao Yazawa**
Translation and English Adaptation **Naoko Amemiya**
Lettering & Touch-Up Art **Walden Wong**
Editor **Eric Searleman**
© 1994 Nao Yazawa/Sukehiro Tomita/Tenyu/Shogakukan.
First published by Shogakukan, Inc.
Japan as "Wedding Peach."

BATTLE ANGEL ALITA: LAST ORDER, VOL. 1 ANGEL REBORN
Story & Art **Yukito Kishiro**
English Adaptation **Fred Burke**
Translation **Lillian Olsen**
Lettering & Touch-Up Art **Susan Daigle-Leach & Adam Symons**
Editor **Annette Roman**
© 2000 by Yukito Kishiro. "Gunnm Last Order" first published in Japan in 2000 by SHUEISHA, INC., Tokyo. English translation rights in the United States and Canada arranged by SHUEISHA Inc. through CLOVERWAY, Inc.

EXCEL SAGA
Story and Art **Rikdo Koshi**
English Adaptation **Dan Kanemitsu & Carl Gustav Horn**
Translation **Dan Kanemitsu**
Lettering & Touch-Up Art **Bruce Lewis**
Editor **Carl Gustav Horn**
EXCEL SAGA © 1997 Rikdo Koshi. Originally published in Japan in 1997 by SHONENGAHOSHA CO., LTD, Tokyo. English translation rights arranged with SHONENGAHOSHA CO., LTD.

PROJECT ARMS: THE FIRST REVELATION: THE AWAKENING
Created **Ryoji Minagawa** and **Kyoichi Nanatsuki**
English Adaptation **Lance Caselman**
Translation **Katy Bridges**
Touch-up Art & Lettering **Bill Schuch**
Editor **Andy Nakatani**
© 1997 Ryoji Minagawa/Kyouchi Nanatsuki/Shogakukan.
First Published by Shogakukan, Inc. in Japan as "ARMS."

TUXEDO GIN
Story and Art **Tokihiko Matsuura**
Translation **Kenichiro Yagi**
Lettering & Touch-Up Art **Adam Symons**
Editor **Andy Nakatani**
©1997 Tokihiko Matsuura/Shogakukan.
First published by Shogakukan, Inc. in Japan as "Takishiido Gin."

FLAME OF RECCA
Story & Art **Nobuyuki Anzai**
English adaptation **Lance Caselman**
Translation **Joe Yamazaki**
Lettering & Touch-Up Art **Kelle Han**
Editor **Eric Searleman**
© 1995 Nobuyuki Anzai/Shogakukan.
First published by Shogakukan, Inc. in Japan as "Recca no Honoo."

GYO
Story & Art **Junji Ito**
English Adaptation **Yuji Oniki**
Lettering & Touch-Up Art **Steve Dutro**
Editors **Alvin Lu** and **Jason Thompson**
© 2002 Junji Ito/Shogakukan.
First published by Shogakukan, Inc. in Japan as "Gyo."

The stories, characters and incidents mentioned in this publication are entirely fictional or are used in an entirely fictional manner.

EXPLANATION OF AGE RATINGS

 Teen May contain violence, language, suggestive situations and alcohol or tobacco usage. Recommended for ages 13 and up.

 Teen Plus Recommended for ages 13+. Possible sexually-oriented nudity (but no explicit sex). No bans on language. Possible gory violence. Mature themes.

 Mature Recommended for ages 18+. Mature themes and depictions.

shô

shô•jo (sho'jo) *n.* **1.** Manga appealing to both female and male readers
2. Exciting stories with true-to-life characters and the thrill of exotic locales
3. Connecting the heart and mind through real human relationships.

Shôjo titles from **VIZ**:

Banana Fish • Basara • Boys over Flowers ~ Hana Yori Dango • Ceres, Celestial Legend
Fushigi Yûgi • Marionette Generation • Please Save My Earth • Revolutionary Girl Utena
Wedding Peach • X/1999

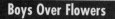

...OH, SHOOT.

DONE! I'M HEADING FOR SCHOOL!

THE STRESS IS GONNA MAKE HER SNAP.

YOU SEND AN AVERAGE GIRL TO AN ELITE SCHOOL...

I'M A *WEED!*

TSUKUSHI... WHAT'S WRONG WITH YOU?

MOM—

YOU CAN PULL A WEED AND MOW IT DOWN... BUT IT ALWAYS GROWS BACK STRONGER THAN EVER!

N-NOOO!

KINDA LOOKS LIKE MARIE ANTOINETTE.

Then one of my assistants said...

WE'LL CALL HIM ANTOINETTE.

Then the other one said...

SHUT UP AND DRAW!

Or I'll beat you up!

"About Tsukasa Domyoji's hairstyle"

This takes up more time than anything. I originally wanted to draw dredlocks, but I just couldn't get them right and they ended up like this.

BRRRR

OH, GEEZ...

...WHAT HAVE I GOTTEN MYSELF INTO...?

IT'S BEEN A LONG TIME SINCE WE HAD ONE THAT SPUNKY.

LET'S REALLY ENJOY IT.

AND NO MERCY JUST BECAUSE SHE'S A GIRL.

DOMYOJI AND NISHIKADO OF THE F4.

GASP

SHHHHHH·····HHH

"AND NO MERCY JUST BECAUSE SHE'S A GIRL."

VSH

I WON'T GO DOWN EASY!

HUH...?

Embarrassing.

GRAND-PA...

IF I STAY IN BED, I'LL **DIE**.

FOOL!

ELDER!

KOF KOF

IT'S STILL A TAD EARLY FOR THAT.

YOU MUSTN'T GET OUT OF BED...

FIRST.

WE MUST DESTROY THE VILLAGE.

WE SET SOME GUNPOWDER IN THE MOUNTAINS FOR JUST SUCH A CASE.

TATARA, WE MUST OBLITER-ATE ALL RECORDS

OF ALL OUR COMMUNI-CATIONS WITH OTHER REBEL VILLAGES.

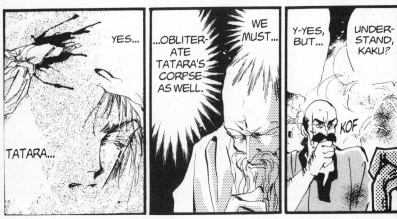

YES...

TATARA...

...OBLITER-ATE TATARA'S CORPSE AS WELL.

WE MUST...

Y-YES, BUT...

UNDER-STAND, KAKU?

KOF

THE MOUNTAIN PASSAGES ARE TREACHEROUS. THE ENEMY WILL NOT HAVE MANNED THEM AS HEAVILY. GET EVERYONE OUT THAT WAY, THEN SET THE GUNPOWDER!

BUT HOW WILL WE GET THERE...?

YES...

KAKU!

YES SIR!

BROTHER.

FATHER.

WE MUST LEAVE YOU HERE...

I CAN'T LET YOU DO THAT!

I WILL RIDE OUT THE FRONT...

DON'T INTERRUPT ME!

THERE IS NO OTHER WAY!

...TO DISTRACT THEM.

BUT...

I HAVEN'T RIDDEN SINCE I WAS LITTLE...

YES!

IS MY HORSE ALIVE?

DO AS TATARA SAYS, KAKU.

Y-YES

SIR...

HOO!

HIIIN

SNORT

WHOA!

EASY!

HE'S LIKE A BROTHER. HEADSTRONG YATO—THE "NIGHT BLADE!"

TATARA SHARED THE MILK OF THIS STALLION'S DAM.

HHF

I CAN'T FALL OFF IN FRONT OF EVERYBODY

I'M TATARA!

YOUR LEGS ARE FASTER THAN ANY STEED OF THE RED KING.

TAKE CARE OF TATARA FOR ME.

YATO.

NAGI?

SHH

TAKE CARE...

...OF TATARA.

MAKOTO'S MOTHER...

GO RUN YOUR HEART OUT, BOY!

PAP

HE'LL BE FINE. I'VE BEEN GETTIN' HIM READY FOR A DAY JUST LIKE THIS!

YES! YES!

LORD TATARA!

LORD TATARA!

TATA-RA.

SARA-SA.

TUG

SWISH

NOW HANG ON TIGHT.

YOU MUST ONLY EVADE THEM.

SNORT

DON'T LET YOUR PASSION SEND YOU CHARGING INTO THEIR MIDST.

...CANNOT PROTECT THE LIVES OF OTHERS.

THOSE WHO DO NOT VALUE THEIR OWN LIVES...

TRUST YATO.

HORSES TRUST THOSE WHO TRUST THEM.

JUST LIKE MY MOTHER.

YOU'RE A NAG, NAGI.

I THINK SHE'S SMILING JUST TO PUT EVERYONE ELSE AT EASE.

DID YOU *SEE* HER?

OH. RIGHT. SORRY.

SHE SMILED...?

OHH!

WE'LL BE SAVED!

HE WAS *SMILING!*

KLP

KLP. KLP

WE'LL BE ALL RIGHT!

KLP

GET THEM INTO THE MOUN-TAINS!

KAKU!

TAKE CARE OF EVERY-ONE!

WAS SHE KILLED!?

KLP KLP

SNIF

SNIF

SOB

I DON'T SEE MOM.

DID THEY TAKE HER AWAY!?

KLP

I HAVE TO HANG ON SO I WON'T BE SHAKEN OFF!

SOB

SOB

I JUST—

I AM TATARA!

I AM THE BOY OF DESTINY.

NO. SHE IS CRYING.

WITH GRIEF AND FEAR.

TATARA!?

I THOUGHT THE GENERAL CUT OFF HIS HEAD!

THE BOY OF DESTINY IS *ALIVE!?*

DM DM DM

LET'S GO!

BUT SLOW! WATCH FOR ARROWS! KEEP YOUR HEADS DOWN!

TATARA'S NAME ALONE PROVIDES A POTENT DECOY.

FINE, FINE! I DIDN'T ASK FOR A SERMON!

"GOD TEMPERS THE WIND TO THE SHORN LAMB."

HEAVEN SHOWS MERCY TO THOSE WHO SHOW MERCY.

HOW CAN YOU STAY SO CALM?

THIS IS KILLING ME!

HUH...?

YOU'RE A MAN!?

ALL RIGHT?

THE HAIR FOOLED ME.

WHAT A DISAPPOINTMENT.

THOUGH I DON'T KNOW WHO YOU ARE...

YES...

CHING

HOO

SEEMS I WAS LATE.

THAT'S AGEHA.

UM... BUTTERFLY...?

WHERE'D YOU POP OUT FROM?

I REMEMBER THOSE BLUE ROBES...

HOO!

SO HE'S STILL ALIVE!

...TATARA? THE BOY OF DESTINY?

TATARA IS IN THE SOUTHERN DESERT!

WILL...

WILL YOU HELP US?

...SIRE?

IT DOESN'T MATTER IF THAT RIDER IS TATARA OR NOT. HE'S A DECOY.

WITH-DRAW THE TROOPS.

CALL THEM BACK.

NOW!

THE VILLAGERS ARE PLOTTING SOMETHING.

BLAM

DEAR GODS,

TSS

PLEASE!

EVERY-BODY, GET BACK!

TSS

GYAAAAAA

DOOM

RRRRRR

BOOM

DMM

KKK

RMMM

...WE'D HAVE LOST *HALF OUR MEN!*

IF THE ORDER HAD CAME A MOMENT LATER...

SUCH A DRASTIC RESPONSE!

S... SWAL-LOWED UP...

WHAT ABOUT THE AUTHENTICITY OF TATARA'S HEAD?

THAT WAY, THEY WILL DIE IN THE DESERT.

PUT OUT A NOTICE TO THE NEIGHBORING VILLAGES.

NO ONE IS TO HELP A SINGLE VILLAGER FROM BYAKKO.

HMM...

THAT'S OUR LEADER!

...ONCE CALLED THE "BOY OF DESTINY" BY PROPHETS.

THE RED KING WAS ALSO...

48

TATARA'S HEAD WILL BE PUT ON DISPLAY.

DO YOU WANT YOUR LIPS SEWN TO-GETHER, ASHO?

ALWAYS SO KIND... TO HORS-ES.

OH NO, SIRE!

BRR!

THE WELL HERE HAS BEEN BURIED,

AND THE HORSES ARE THIRSTY.

BACK TO LIGHT-HOUSE FORT.

KLP KLP KLP

AND PROVE TO THE WHOLE COUNTRY THE BOY OF DESTINY IS A MYTH!

HUH?

...OF COURSE!

POM

KLP

KMM

RMM

THEY USED TO SAY...

...THAT A DEMON LIVES IN THE LAND OF IRON.

FT ITS FOOTPRINTS HERE.

TODAY, A RED DEMON...

TO BE CONTINUED IN VOL. I

Wedding Peach

Created by Sukehiro Tomita

Story and Art by Nao Yazawa

Tough love wa,
never this cute

shōjo

MAGICAL GIRL HEROINES UNITE TO SAVE THE WORLD

MANGA BASED ON THE POPULAR JAPANESE TV SHOW AND VIDEO SERIES

Wedding Peach

Created by **Sukehiro Tomita**
Story and Art by **Nao Yazawa**

Vol. 1

RATED
T
TEEN

Armed with magical powers borne from age-old wedding ceremony traditions, Momoko suddenly finds herself in a perilous position. She must battle a pair of ruthless demons who want to rid the earth of love and sweetness. It doesn't take her long to realize that she can't save the world all by herself. Thank goodness the young schoolgirl has friends like Yuri and Hinagiku. Introducing Wedding Peach, Angel Lily and Angel Daisy: three angelic warriors who aren't afraid to kick booty and look cute at the same time.

Bimonthly

$9.95

Available in Au

I SHALL *NOT* ALLOW IT!

that is my ento ama!

ON THIS ELEGANT GREEN CAMPUS WHERE CHERRY BLOSSOMS FLOWER, MANY FRIENDS LIE UNCONSCIOUS BECAUSE OF YOU!

RAUSCH

NOKO!

HOLD IT!

BOOOM

YEAH?

I SHALL MAKE BLOSSOM THE POWER OF LOVE!

THE LILY REPRESENTS PURITY...

I'LL BLOW AWAY THE WINDS OF EVIL!!

THE DAISY – A SYMBOL OF INNOCENCE.

WHAT
IS THAT
...
THAT
LIGHT!?

ISONER of Society.

ORDSMAN Without Equal.

A GIRL With A Dream.

itten and Illustrated by
IHO SAITO

y by
-PAPAS

Revolutionary Girl UTENA

As seen in

VIZ

action

ac•tion (ak′shən) *n.* **1.** To initiate or proceed. **2.** A responsibility, mission, duty. **3.** To move or advance towards change, as in an attempt to better a situation or environment. **4.** A call to battle between good and evil.

Action titles from **VIZ**:

The All-New Tenchi Muyô! • Bastard!! • Battle Angel Alita • The Big O • DiGi Charat • Excel Saga • Firefighter!: Daigo of Fire Company M • Flame of Recca • Gundam • Inu-Yasha • Medabots • Neon Genesis Evangelion • Project Arms • Ranma 1/2 • Short Program • Silent Möbius • Steam Detectives • No Need For Tenchi! • Tuxedo Gin • Video Girl Ai • ZOIDS

WHAT HAPPENED HERE?!

WE'LL TELL YOU THE DETAILS AFTER YOU MEET OUR LEADER.

THAT'S WHY WE NEED YOUR HELP!

THINGS ARE BAD RIGHT NOW...

...I'M BUSY.

HOLD ON A SEC'...

ALL KIDS... NO GROWN-UPS...

EEK! IT SEES US!

QUICK! GET DOWN!

PHEW...

fmp

WOW.

IS IT *REAL*?

WONDER WHAT IT *EATS*...

DON'T PUSH!

DOES IT HAVE LASER VISION?

kreek

glub

...YOU LOOK DIFFERENT FROM THE LAST TIME I SAW YOU—*IN THE LAB.*

WOW...

ALITA IS A CYBORG FROM THE SURFACE...

OKAY, LISTEN UP!

oooh!

SHE HAS A *BRAIN!*

SHE HAS A *BRAIN!*

...BUT SHE HAS A *BRAIN!*

pap

WHICH MEANS SHE'S ONE OF *US!*

MY NAME'S JIM ROSCOE.

I NEVER SAID I'D JOIN YOU.

SO HE KNOWS NOVA!

I WAS IN PROFESSOR NOVA'S LAB WHEN...I SAW HIM REGENERATE YOUR BRAIN WITH MY OWN EYES!

...AND IT'S *NOT* LIKE WHAT'S INSIDE *ADULT* SKULLS *HERE.*

YOU *ARE* ONE OF US.

I SAW WHAT'S IN YOUR *SKULL,* ALITA...

SHE HAS A *BRAIN!*

SHE HAS A *BRAIN!*

88

...THE *SECRET* OF THE *TIPHAREANS*?

SO YOU *KNOW?* YOU FOUND OUT...

YEAH... SO I *SEE*...

BRAIN!

BRAIN!

IT'S NOT MUCH OF A SECRET THESE DAYS.

UH-HUH.

DO YOU FEEL BETTER, PAM?

...SINCE THE WORD GOT OUT.

IT'S BEEN A ROUGH WEEK, ALITA. *EVERYTHING* HAS CHANGED...

THIS WAS RIGHT AFTER WE REBUILT YOUR BODY.

mnch

LAST WEEK, PROFESSOR NOVA HI-JACKED THE WHOLE TIPHAREAN BROADCAST NETWORK— EVERY SINGLE MONITOR.

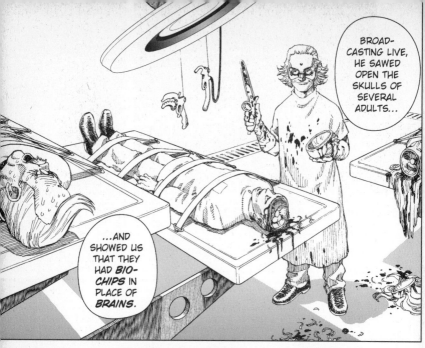

BROADCASTING LIVE, HE SAWED OPEN THE SKULLS OF SEVERAL ADULTS...

...AND SHOWED US THAT THEY HAD *BIO-CHIPS* IN PLACE OF *BRAINS*.

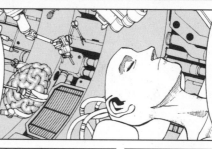

...BUT NO ONE GUESSED WHAT WAS *REALLY* INVOLVED! AT AGE NINETEEN, OUR BRAINS ARE *REPLACED* WITH BIO-CHIPS—DIGITAL COPIES OF OUR *MEMORIES*. IT WAS *M.I.B.'S* DIRTIEST SECRET...

WE ALL KNEW THAT WE HAD TO UNDERGO AN INITIATION TO BECOME FULL-FLEDGED CITIZENS OF TIPHARES...

I WAS IN SHOCK, TOO, OF COURSE. SO...

...I WENT TO THE LAB...

M.I.B. ROBOTS, PROGRAMMED TO COVER UP THE TRUTH, WENT ON A KILLING SPREE.

...AND IT DIDN'T GO OVER TOO WELL.

RIOTS, INSANITY, SUICIDE... CHAOS ENSUED.

...AND KILLED PROFESSOR NOVA, JUST TO *SEE*.

SUDDENLY THE CLOUDINESS, THE THOUGHTS I DIDN'T UNDERSTAND...THEY ALL FELL INTO PLACE...

...AND I *REALIZED* WHAT I WANTED.

HERE. LOOK.

......

DID HE HAVE A BIO-CHIP IN *HIS* HEAD TOO?

SURE ENOUGH, THERE IT WAS.

THE PROFESSOR'S BIO-CHIPS. THEY'RE MINE NOW.

THE SECOND ONE IS THE BACKUP FROM HIS STOMACH...

klink

MIB

WE HAVE 235 CHILDREN IN THIS STRONG-HOLD...

NO.

GIMME ONE.

EIGHTY PERCENT OF ALL TIPHARES LOST IN **ONE WEEK**...

JIM HACKED INTO THE M.I.B. COMPUTER TO STOP THE FLOW OF KILLER ROBOTS...

...BUT THERE ARE STILL A LOT OF ASSASSIN MACHINES ROAMING AROUND OFFLINE*.

slrp

OUR SCOUTS SAY 4000 SANE ADULTS SURVIVE ON THE OTHER SIDE OF TIPHARES.

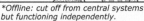

*Offline: cut off from central systems but functioning independently.

93

BUT WE'LL CLEAN UP...

...GET RID OF THE BRAINLESS HUMAN *POSERS*, AND MAKE TIPHARES *OUR* CITY... *OUR* HOME!

GUESS YOU DON'T KNOW...

YOU MEAN OUR C.C.M.'S*?

HUH?

WHAT BECAME OF YOUR *PARENTS*?

...I'D *STILL* SAY, "KILL THEM ALL!"

NO DNA BINDS US, BUT IF IT *DID*...

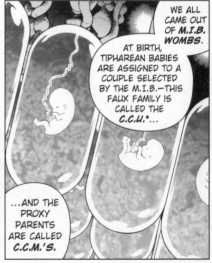

WE ALL CAME OUT OF *M.I.B. WOMBS.*

AT BIRTH, TIPHAREAN BABIES ARE ASSIGNED TO A COUPLE SELECTED BY THE M.I.B.—THIS FAUX FAMILY IS CALLED THE *C.C.U.**...

...AND THE PROXY PARENTS ARE CALLED *C.C.M.'S.*

*C.C.M.: Child Care Manager
*C.C.U.: Child Care Unit

94

 ...A FRIEND WHOSE BRAIN WAS TRADED IN FOR A BIO-CHIP.

BUT SHE'S DIFFERENT— SHE BROKE TIPHAREAN RULES TO SAVE MY LIFE.

 THERE'S SOMEONE I HAVE TO LOOK FOR....

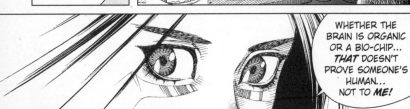 WHETHER THE BRAIN IS ORGANIC OR A BIO-CHIP... *THAT* DOESN'T PROVE SOMEONE'S HUMAN... NOT TO *ME*!

 ...YOUR OPINION. WHAT SHOULD WE BELIEVE?

YES. I'D LIKE TO HEAR...

 THEN WHAT *DOES* IT MEAN... TO BE HUMAN?

WELL, THAT'S NOT *MY* PROBLEM...

...WHAT'S GOING TO HAPPEN TO THEM NOW?

...BUT THESE POOR, MIXED-UP KIDS...

TIPHARES NEVER MADE SENSE TO BEGIN WITH...

NO USE TRYING TO STOP ME.

THAT'S NOT WHY...

HFF

UFF

UFF HFF

WAIT UP!

AW, BUT...

ME! NOT *YOU*, PAM!

JIM TOLD ME TO BE YOUR GUIDE...

ARE YOU SURE ABOUT THIS?

MAYBE I SHOULD GO, TOO! ISN'T NOLA IN DANGER?

THAT'S NOT WHAT I MEANT, JIM...

THE MORE DANGER...

...THE *BETTER.*

WHAT A SURPRISE. I WAS *POSITIVE* SHE WOULD JOIN US...

...BUT WE STILL HOLD THE TRUMP CARD.

...GETS HURT, OR EVEN DIES...

...ALITA'S FAILURE TO PROTECT HER WILL MAKE HER FEEL INDEBTED TO US...

heh

ALITA IS BOUND BY HER SENSE OF DUTY.

AS LONG AS SHE'S TRYING TO PROTECT NOLA, SHE WON'T JOIN FORCES WITH OUR ENEMY.

AND IF NOLA...

HE... HE CAN'T BE *SERIOUS*...

MY PRECIOUS *MONSTER* IS ABOUT TO BE *BORN*...

C'MON! LET'S GET READY FOR OUR VISIT TO THE M.I.B. CENTRAL CORE!

TO BE CONTINUED IN VOL. I

TO *THINK* THAT AN *UNDERGROUND HEADQUARTERS* WOULD POSSESS SUCH A *WEAKNESS*...

...IT WAS SOMETHING I HAD NOT *FORESEEN*.

WELL, WELL...

UGM... *WYEATH!*

UGM...

WHAT DO *YOU* MAKE OF THIS SITUATION, *EXCEL?*

WELL, SIR, IN ORDER TO KINDLE SOME FAINT SEMBLANCE OF *HOPE* AMIDST THESE *DIRE CIRCUMSTANCES*, I FELT EAGER -- EVEN COMPELLED -- TO SEND SOME *DECOYS* FLOATNG FORTH...

got lightheaded for a moment

YOU CERTAINLY ARE *FOND* OF THOSE THINGS, *AREN'T* YOU?

106

ANY IDEAS ON *SPECIFIC STEPS* TO BE TAKEN TO ENRICH THE HEARTS OF CHILDREN?

SIR!

CHILDREN WITH *ENRICHED HEAR* WILL BECOME *ENLIGHTENE* CITIZENS...

..*ENLIGHTENED CITIZENS* WILL UNDOUBTEDLY ACCEPT THE RULERSHIP OF THE *RIGHTEOUS LEADER.*

I HUMBLY SUGGEST— SHALL WE NOT ATTEMPT TO IMPROVE THE QUALITY OF THE HOT SCHOOL LUNCH?!?

SIR! ENRICHED HEARTS FROM ENRICHED MEALS!

GO AHE

ACK

CITY CONQUEST PLAN #1154

YES. REALIZE THAT IT WAS MY SUGGESTION... YET -- SOMEHOW-- I FIND THAT I MUST CONCUR.

DO YOU NOT THINK RATHER THAT IT IS AN *IMPOSSIBLE* IDEA?

school an't even ke curry ste good...

NO, I DO NOT THINK IT IS A BAD IDEA...

WAS IT... A... *BAD* IDEA?

HM?

MOVING ON TO THE *NEXT* PLAN...

DON'T YOU FEEL...

LORD IL PA*LAZZO,* IT'S TIME FOR ME TO GO TO *WORRRKK...*

I ABSOLUTELY, UTTERLY, COMPLETELY, THOROUGHLY *DO NOT* THINK SO...

heh, heh

slightly confident

...THAT THERE I SOMETHI *MISSIN* TODAY:

PULL TO PURGE ENEMIES

welp, gotta be on my way...

JUST LOOK AT ALL THE *STUFF* THAT'S FLOATING ABOUT...

OKAY *WON*

...AND OVER THERE, A *PUPPY* BEING WASHED AWAY...

YELP! YAP! HYAP!

LOOKS LIKE TH COLONE MAKING DELIVER DOWN T *DAVY JONES LOCKER*

MM HMM!

Dog
→ Organism
→ **EDIBLE**

PUPPY?

111

I MEAN, I HARDLY *EVER* GET HUNGRY ENOUGH TO EAT A *DOG!* ✳

AH-HA HA HA!

KIDDING! I'M ONLY KIDDING! ...

✳ WHICH IMPLIES THAT THERE ARE TIMES WHEN SHE DOES.

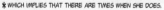

HUH?

BI-*CYC*-LE!
BI-*CYC*-LE!

BI—

AWW... I'LL GIVE YOU A NICE *TREAT* WHEN I'M DONE WORKING...

stolen — with the finesse of a cat burglar!

"*stolen*"?

gone in sixty seconds... or maybe less!

...and almost certainly by a state-sponsored conspiracy!

but... it isn't stolen...

I SHALL **NOT** BE DEFEATED!

BUT DON'T **WORRY**, PUPPY!

...I CANNOT LET SOME prettybicyclethief STATE CONSPIRACY DEFEAT ME NOW!

WITH DAWN OVER A CONQUERED CITY FAST APPROACHING...

HA HA HA HA HA HA

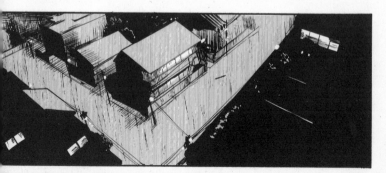

HEY, MY CELL PHONE...

I *SAID* I'M NOT THE ONE WHO'S *DOIN'* IT, DAMMIT!

SHUT *UP!* *YOU'RE* THE ONE THAT'S ALWAYS LETTING OUT THOSE WEIRD *SCREAMS!*

NO, I'M *NOT* THE--

RIGHT?

i give up...

IT SURE IS A *SCARY* WORLD, HUH? *ROUGH* AND *TOUGH* OUT THERE...

YES?...

...HT *NOW?*...

...I ...PERSTAND, SIR....

...BE THERE ...IICKLY...!

HEY, IT STOPPED.

ACK!

OH, THE NOISE? PLEASE DON'T LET IT BOTHER YOU...

YES, WHO *IS* IT?

OH, LORD *IL PALAZZO!*

YES? WHAT CAN I *DO* FOR YOU...?

WHAT *WAS* IT? SOUNDED LIKE SOMEONE DUMPING THEIR *TRASH* ON THE GROUND...

HUH?

THAT WAS QUITE FAST.

HAIL

PALAZZO

LOOKS LIKE THE *WATER LEVEL'S* GONE UP QUITE A BIT...

WOW...

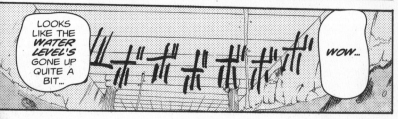

OH, I JUST *FOUND* HER.

HER NAME IS *MINCE*...

BY THE WAY, WHY IS THERE A *DOG* ON YOUR HEAD?

YES, WE CERTAINLY MUST DO SOMETHING...

WHY DON'T WE *DO* SOMETHING, LORD IL PALAZZO?

ACK!

--AND *EXECUTIVE OFFICER*, AND *STAFF OFFICER*, AND HAVE *YOU* BE THE *LATRINE ORDERLY*?

SIR, W DON'T GO AHE AND HA HER BE ACROS COMBAT

UM, OUR SECRET ACRO HEADQUARTER ...IT *IS* EQUIPPED W A *BATHROO* ISN'T IT?

YES, WHAT *ABOUT* IT?

I'M THINKING... THIS *BATHROOM* MUST BE MESSED UP *BAD*, WHAT WITH ALL THIS FLOODING...

AND NOT ONLY DID I *SWIM* IN THIS, BUT I *DRANK* SOME OF THIS...

...must-use-proper-syntax...!

AND... REAL TENSE SITUATION THIS... UM, IS... AND...

WHOOOOOAAAAAAAAAAAAAAAAA!

YOU NEVER CEASE TO *MAZE*, LORD IL PALAZZO!

THAT'S *JUST* WHAT I WAS *THINKING* OF!

YES! EXACTLY!

LIKE A *FLUSH* TOILET?

LORD IL PALAZZO!

THIS LOOKS AWFULLY FAMILIAR!

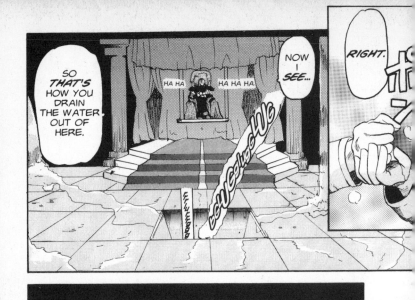

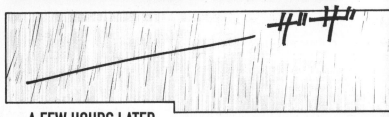

A FEW HOURS LATER

I WONDER WHAT *COUNTRY* THEY'RE ALL FROM...?

BOY, WE SURE *LUCKED OUT--* HAVING THIS HELPFUL *SHIP* PASS BY US, MINCE...

i might have died there...

I SURE DIDN'T KNOW THAT OUR *UNDERGROUND HEADQUARTERS* WAS CONNECTED TO THE *OCEAN...*

LOCAL STATIONS! WE MUST BE *CLOSE* TO SHORE!

YES!

this well-developed depression

expected to pass through western Japan and into the Pacific

OH! A *RADIO!*

THIS EPISODE'S SLAVES: YOKOMAEBA CHIMPATSU AND KINEMA (EVERYBODY LOVES INSECT

...the immigration Bureau has begun immediate investigation, with much concern over the international implications of...

WELL, *WELL.*

...a ship carrying illegal immigrants was intercepted by the Japanese Coast Guard while approaching the coast in the pre-dawn hours of this morning...

LET'S SEE... WHAT *NEWS* FROM THE WORLD TODAY....

TV12

THE GLOBE IS *YET AGAIN* IN *TURMOIL.*

カチャ

HOW *DISAPPOINTING.*

IN ANY CASE, *EXCEL* SEEMS TO BE *TARDY*...

Immigration Bureau

I MUST COMPLIMENT YOU UPON YOR *MASTERY* OF THE JAPANESE LANGUAGE...

...YOUR *AGE*...?

UNSPECIFIED!

YOUR *NAME*?

I CAN REVEAL MY *CODE* NAME...

NATIONALITY?

SECRET.

カッカッ

ND MISSION 2

TO BE CONTINUED IN VOL. 1

104.1.1 FX: ZUDODODODODO [zZgUSHuSHuSHuSH (sound, water gushing in at a thunderous pace)]

104.1.2 FX: (next to Il Palazzo) HAHAHA (sound, laughter)]

105.1 FX: JABABABABA [wISHISHISHISH (sound, water gushing out like a powerful shower head)]

105.2 FX: DABABABABA [thPLaSHpLAshPlaSHpLAsh (sound, large flow of water, thrashing down)]

105.3 FX: PUSUUU [phffft (sound, Excel blowing into decoy)]

105.4 FX: BODODODODODO [phVLupVLupVLupVLup (sound, water pouring down)]

106.4 FX: BUNBUKUGUKUKU [blub blub blub (sound, air being pushed out of the submerged decoys)]

106.5 FX: TERE TERE [blush blush (depiction, Excel somewhat embarrassed at her own answer)]

107.3.1 FX: CHAPPU [spLAsh (sound, water)]

107.3.2 FX: BASHAN [zPLosssh (sound, water)]

107.3.3 FX: TEYA "HUMPH" (depiction, Excel lunging out)]

107.3.4 FX: BASHAN [zPLosssh (sound, water)]

107.5.1 FX: PON [fumpht (sound, stamping sound)]

107.5.2 FX: GAAAN ["sound" of shock]

108.2 FX: CHAPUN [sCHtn (sound, water)]

108.3 FX: ZIRIRIRI RIRIRIRI [b'ringringring ringringringring . . . (sound, alarm ring)]

108.4 FX: RIRI RIRI [ringring (sound, alarm ring)]

108.5 FX: RIN... [ring... (sound, alarm ring cut off)]

109.1.1 FX: PURAAAN PURAAAN [swing swing (depiction, rope and swinging back and forth)]

109.1.2 FX: DAPA DAPA DAPA [thPlaSHaPlaSHaPlasha (sound, fluttering kicking motion against water)]

109.1.3 FX: UFUHE [thehehe (sound, Excel laughing but somewhat nervously)]

109.2.1 FX: BUKUKUKU [blub blub blub (depiction, submerging)]

109.2.2 FX: DOZAZAAA [zZgUSHuSHuSHuSHuSH (sound, water gushing in at a thunderous pace)]

109.3 FX: ZA ZAAAA [z'ZSHSHSHSHhh (sound, strong pouring rain)]

109.4 FX: ZABOZOBOZABO [z'zGuSHGLuSHGLuSH (sound, huge amount of water moving about)]

110.1 FX: JABU JAPO [thrPLAsh SuPLAsh (sound, cutting through water)]

110.2 FX: UZAZAZAZA [z'ZSHSHSHSHhh (sound, cutting through water)]

110.3.1 FX: KI [skreach (sound, brake sound)]

110.3.2 FX: CHAPAN [sCHtn (sound, water sound)]

110.4 FX: KATAN [k'Lunk (sound, metal gate opening through flap)]

111.1 FX: ZUMOMOMOMO [z'ZnZnZnZnNNN (depiction, large object floating by)]

111.2 FX: DONBURAAA DOBURAAA [bobin' bobin' (depiction, the state of objects floating down the river)]

111.3 FX: KYAN! HYAN! HYAN! [yelp! Hyap! Hyap! (sound, cute dog barking)]

111.6.1 FX: BOSO [murmur (sound, murmuring speech)]

111.6.2 FX: BIKU ["sound" of a flinch (depiction, flinch)]

112.3.1 FX: GYAN! GYAFU GYAN [yuff yuff yuff (sound, cute dog bark)]

112.3.2 FX: POTO BOTOTO [drppl drppl (sound and depiction, water dropping)]

112.4 FX: POTA POTA [drppl drppl (sound and depiction, water dripping)]

113.1 FX: ZABU ZABU [thrPLAsh SuPLAsh (sound, cutting through water)]

113.2 FX: ZAAAA [z'ZSHSHSHSHhh (sound, strong pouring rain)]

113.3 FX: ZAAAA [z'ZSHSHSHSHhh (sound, strong pouring rain)]

113.6 FX: ZUZOZAZAZA [z'ZwSHwSHSHSHSHhh (sound, noisily being pushed away by water)]

114.1 FX: GYU [ggrip (depiction, fastening something tight or closing a grip on something)]

114.2 FX: ZAN [z'ZRrrip (depiction, dramatic fastening something tight or closing a grip on something)]

114.3 FX: BUZAZAZAZA [z'ZSHSHSHSHhh (sound, cutting through water)]

114.4.1 FX: (to left and right of 114.4.2) BASHA BASHA [thrPLAsh SuPLAsh (sound, cutting through water)]

114.4.2 FX: AAHAHAHAHA [Excel's laughter]

115.1 FX: PATAN [b'THMP (sound, door closing)]

115.3 FX: ZEEEE ZEEEE [sound of Mince's wheezing]

115.4 FX: GOSHI GOSHI [rubb rub (depiction, drying Mince off with towel)]

115.8.1 FX: GAKO [k'CLUNK (knife rock)]

115.8.2 FX: GYARIN [sSHINEee (depiction, dramatic presentation of shiny metallic object)]

116.1.1 FX: KASSHAN [KRASH (sound, something breaking)]

116.1.2 FX: PARIIN [k'SHArrrk (sound, glass shattering)]

116.1.3 FX: GYOON GYAN [Ryuff yRyff (sound, cute dog bark)]

116.1.4 FX: DOSUN [b'Thump (sound, thud sound)]

116.2.1 FX: KATA KATA [klunk klunk (sound, the metal kettle moving about)]

116.2.2 FX: DOSUSUN [b'Thrthump (sound, thud sound)]

116.2.3 FX: DONGARARA [k'shuNK (sound, things shattering apart as it falls down)]

116.2.4 FX: DOGA [bBANG (sound, something hitting)]

116.2.5 FX: GYOO [Ryuff (sound, cute dog bark)]

116.2.6 FX: KYAN [yuff (sound, cute dog whine)]

116.3.1 FX: GYAN [Ryuff (sound, cute dog bark)]

116.3.2 FX: KASHAAAN [k'shuNK (sound, things shattering apart as it falls down)]

116.3.3 FX: DOSU! [b'Thump (sound, thud sound)]

116.3.4 FX: GYAHOHOON [Ryuffffff (sound, cute dog whine)]

116.4.1 FX: (white, above hand) KARAN [k'lunk (depiction, object rolling about)]

116.4.2 FX: (under hand) KU [Ggripp (depiction, gripping)]

116.4.3 FX: GASHAA [k'shuNK (sound, things shattering apart as it falls down)]

116.4.4 FX: KYAN [yuff (sound, cute dog whine)]

116.5 FX: GOGAGOGA GOGAN [bang thud bash crash (sound, fierce flailing about)]

117.1 FX: GACHA k'chunk (sound, door opening)]

117.3 FX: ZUKA ZUKA ZUKA ZUKA [ZhZ ZhZ ZhZ ZhZ (depiction, striding strong, forceful motion)]

117.4 FX: BOKAN! [k'POW! (sound and depiction, thunderous punch)]

118.1.1 FX: GESU [g'THunk (sound and depiction, a jabbing motion)]

118.1.2 FX: BAKI! [kRAck! (sound and depiction, something being broken or similar)]

118.1.3 FX: DOSUN! [THUD (sound, heavy impact)]

118.2 FX: PIROPIROPIRON [pringpringpring (sound, cute phone ring)]

118.3 FX: PIROPIROPIRON pringpringpring (sound, cute phone ring)]

118.4.1 FX: PI [pip (sound, electronic peep sound)]

118.4.2 FX: ZUGAZUGA [kTHdTHd (sound, repeated hits)]

118.4.3 FX: DOKAN [k'THUD (sound, impact)]

118.4.4 FX: GAKON [kLUNK (sound, something being knocked about)]

118.4.5 FX: GUSHA [sk'MAsh (sound, something being smashed)]

118.4.6 FX: SHIIIIN [nNNN (depiction, sound stopping)]

118.4.7 FX: PU [pip (sound, electronic peep sound)]

118.5 FX: GAKAN KAN KAN [kANg kANg kANg (sound, metallic)]

118.6 FX: GASA [k'Zthnk (sound and depiction, something moving after being hit)]

118.7 FX: KO [k'ng (sound, metallic tap)]

119.1.1 FX: KAN KAN KAN [kANg kANg kANg (sound, metallic)]

119.1.2 FX: ZA ZAAAAAA [z'ZSHSHSHhh (sound, strong pouring rain)]

119.3 FX: GO GO GO GO GO GO GO [G'GvRvRvR (sound and depiction, heavy desolate feeling)]

119.4 FX: KOOOOO [mmm m mm m (sound, ambient-large not very personable hall feel)]

119.5-6 FX: BOKOPOKOKOKOKOKO [blublublublublbbbb (sound, bubbling)]

120.1.1 FX: JAPO (white) sCHtn (sound, water sound)

120.1.2 FX: POPUN [(black, small) ch'splch (sound, bursting out)]

120.2.1 FX: CHAPUN CHAPUN [sCHtn sCHtn (sound, water sound)]

120.2.2 FX: GEHO KEHO [(near bottom word balloon) cough cough (Excel coughing)]

120.2.3 FX: BURU BURU PURUN [SHAKE SHAKE SHAKE (movement, shaking head violently)]

120.2.4 FX: GEHO [cough (sound, Excel coughing)]

120.3 FX: BOBOBOBOBOBODO [phVLupVLupVLupVLup (sound, water pouring down)]

120.5.1 FX: CHAPU [sCHtn (sound, water sound)]

120.5.2 FX: CHAPUN [sCHtn (sound, water sound)]

121.2 FX: HA [GASP! (depiction and sound)]

121.4 FX: ZAAAAA [z'ZSHSHSHShhh (sound, strong pouring rain, but also water generally)]

121.5 FX: ZAZAAAAA [z'ZSHSHSHSHhh (sound, strong pouring rain)]

121.6.1 FX: (black) JABU JABU [thrPLAsh SuPLAsh (sound, cutting through water)]

121.6.2 FX: (white) GAKON [k'CLUNK (sound, something being activated)]

122.1 FX: DOGOGO [z'ZngUSHuSHuSHuSH (depiction, massive water flow)]

122.2 FX: GOOOOO [gUSHuSHuSHuSH (flow)]

122.3 FX: APU JABUN [z'thrPLAsh z'SuPLAsh (sound, cutting through water, strong)]

122.5 FX: JUGOGOOO [z'ZngUSHuSHuSHnrUrRuKR (sound, massive flush)]

122.6-7 FX: OOOO [rRRRORR (sound, roaring sound)]

123.1 FX: PON [fumpht (sound, stamping sound)]

123.2.1 FX: HAHAHAHAHA [laughter]

123.2.2 FX: BOGOBOGOGOBORUBORUBORU [b'gluglugluglug... (sound, bubbling flush)]

123.2.3 FX: RURORORO— [mlurrr... (sound, last gurgling sound)]

123.4 FX: ZA ZAAAAA [z'ZSHSHSHSHhh (sound, strong pouring rain)]

123.5.1 FX: ZAZAAAN [z'pLAsh (sound, crashing waves)]

123.5.2 FX: ZAPAAAN [sSpLAsh (sound, crashing waves)]

124.1.1 FX: DODODODODO [vGvGvGvGvG (sound, heavy engine)]

124.1.2 FX: ZUZAZA [z'thrPLAsh z'SuPLAsh (sound, cutting through water, strong)]

124.2.1 FX: ZA ZAZAZAZAZA— [thrPLAsh SuPLAsh... (sound cutting through water)]

124.2.2 FX: DO DO [vGvGvG (sound, heavy engine)]

124.5.1 FX: GAGA [(in upper word balloon) hZzrk (sound static)]

124.5.2 FX: ZUGAGA [(outside lower word balloon) zRrk (static)]

124.5.3 FX: GAGAGA [(in lower word balloon) ZzHrK (static)]

124.6.1 FX: OO [ROAR (sound and depiction)]

124.6.2 FX: WAA [RAAA (sound and depiction)]

125.1.1 FX: WAAAA [rROARr (sound and depiction)]

125.1.2 FX: PIII PIII [phPHIII—' (sound, whistling)]

125.1.3 FX: WAAAA [Raaa (sound and depiction)]

125.1.4 FX: OOOOO [ROAR (sound and depiction)]

125.2.1 FX: ZA ZAAA [z'ZSHSHSHSHhh (sound, strong pouring rain)]

125.2.2 FX: WAAA WAAA WAAA [Rah rah rah (sound and depiction)]

125.2.3 FX: ZAAAA [z'ZSHSHSHSHhh (sound, strong pouring rain)]

125.3 FX: SAAAAAAAAA... [z'ZSHSHSHSHhh (sound, strong pouring rain)]

126.1.1 FX: BUN [WWMm (sound and depiction, electronic screen appearing)]

126.1.2 FX: KACHI [click (sound)]

126.5 FX: KATSU KATSU [scribble scribble (sound and depiction)]

HURRY UP AND GET OUT OF HERE!

I'LL TAKE CARE OF HIM.

SINCE I GOT YOU INTO THIS MESS, I'M GOING TO HELP YOU GET OUT OF IT!

129

No.4 ACTIVATION

...

DIDN'T YOU SEE THEIR *ARMS!?*

YOU CAN'T KEEP UP WITH THOSE GUYS!!

ARE YOU OUT OF YOUR MIND!?

I DON'T EVEN THINK THAT THEY'RE HUMAN! THEY'RE DEMONS OR SOMETHING!

THEY WERE DEADLY WEAPONS!!

I'M NEVER LEAVING HOME WITHOUT MY CELL PHONE AGAIN!

THE BEST WE CAN DO FOR HAYATO IS TO GET OUT OF HERE AND CALL THE POLICE!

!

THEY LOOK LIKE THEY'RE ENGINEERS OR SOMETHING...

SEE THOSE GUYS DOWN THERE?

WHY NOT!?

I DON'T THINK WE'RE GOING ANY-WHERE...

BUT THEY'RE CARRYING SOME SCARY LOOKING WEAPONS...

I DON'T THINK THAT THEY'RE GOING TO LET US OUT OF HERE...

SO...

TO THINK THAT THE OTHER ARMS WOULD RUN AWAY...

YOU KNOW, I ALMOST FEEL SORRY FOR YOU.

LOOKS LIKE WE'VE GOT TO FIGHT CLAW WHETHER WE LIKE IT OR NOT.

YOU...

YOU GUYS ARE LIKE FISH... I MEAN ARMS... IN A BARREL. HEH HEH...

OUR PEOPLE HAVE THIS PLACE SURROUNDED.

BUT THOSE TWO WON'T GET VERY FAR...

THAT'S IT... GET ANGRY!

BASTARD!!

YOU...

OOF

THAT'S THE DIFFERENCE BETWEEN A *PROFESSIONAL* AND AN *AMATEUR.* HAVE YOU LEARNED YOUR LESSON YOUNG MAN?

OH, DEAR. YOUR ATTACK WAS TOO RECKLESS-- NOW YOU'VE GOT A BOO-BOO.

UGH... UHRR...

I GUESS THE QUALITY OF OUR AGENTS HAS SIGNIFICANTLY DROPPED IF THEY CAN BE BEATEN BY THE LIKES OF YOU.

!!

SO YOU'RE THE FEARSOME HAYATO SHINGU, WHO KILLED FIVE OF THE ORGANIZATION'S AGENTS. WELL, WELL...

RYO... IS THIS REALLY HAPPENING TO US?

IS HE TRYING TO MAKE A FOOL OF *ME!?*

AND THE HORO-SCOPE FOR CANCER WASN'T SO GREAT EITHER, RYO....

I SHOULD HAVE KNOWN. MY HOROSCOPE SAID IT WOULD BE A BAD WEEK FOR ME...

I'M REALLY SCARED AND CONFUSED TOO.

I'M TOO SCARED TO EVEN THINK.

THINGS ARE SO CRAZY YET YOU'RE ABLE TO BE CALM AND COLLEC-TED.

YOU KNOW RYO, YOU'RE REALLY AMAZING...

"TO WIN, YOU HAVE TO **KNOW** YOUR SURROUNDINGS AND USE WHATEVER'S AVAILABLE."

BUT MY DAD ALWAYS SAID-- "YOU CAN'T WIN IF YOU LOSE YOUR COOL."

I NEVER THOUGHT THE TRAPS AND THE SURVIVAL STUFF DAD DRILLED INTO ME WOULD COME IN AS HANDY AS THEY HAVE.

IT'S LIKE HE WAS PREPARING ME... LIKE HE KNEW THIS DAY WOULD COME...

140

SO I'LL JUST HAVE TO VENT MY ANGER SOMEWHERE ELSE!

UN-FORTUNATELY HEAD-QUARTERS WANTS ALL OF YOU *ARMS* KIDS CAPTURED ALIVE.

I'D PREFER TO RIP OUT YOUR SPLEEN RIGHT HERE...

....

BEFORE I DISABLE YOU, I'M GONNA REMODEL YOUR PRETTY LITTLE FRIEND'S FACE BEFORE YOUR VERY EYES!

...THIS'LL DO...

TOUGH GUYS LIKE YOU CAN HANDLE TORTURE... BUT YOU ALWAYS BREAK DOWN WHEN YOUR FRIENDS ARE IN PAIN. HEH HEH...

KATSUMI!!!

THEN YOU SHALL HAVE POWER!!

WHAT'S HAPPENING TO ME!?

WHA--?

TO BE CONTINUED IN VOL. I

129.1	KA KA KA KA: running FX
129.3	KA KA: running FX
134.1	BASHU BA: wak whoosh
134.2	DA: tmp
134.3	JAKI: fwk
134.4	GASHU: slish
135.1	ZUN: thud
135.3	GA: fwump
135.4	GURI GURI: skrunch skrunch
135.6	DO: thunk
136.3	The graffiti on the wall is a tribute to Argentine soccer legend Diego Maradona.
137.2	ZUSHU: shunk [pulling out spear]
137.3	GA: thwak
137.6	BAFUN: [stepping on something]
138.2	DOGAKAN: crash
138.3	BIN BIIN: twang
138.4	GUGU: clatter
138.5	ZUN: [coming out from the dust]
139.1	CHOKICHOKI: snip snip
139.2	CHOKICHOKI: snip snip
139.6	GYU GYU: bend bend
140.1	GYU GYU: stretch stretch
141.1	KIRI KIRI: stretch stretch
141.3	MEKI: crack
141.4	DOGA: crash
142.2	HYUU: thwizz
142.3	BASU: thunk
142.5	ZUBU: [pulling out arrow]
142.6	MEKI: crack
143.3	GA: grab
143.4	JAKIN: shwik
144.3	PI: slish
145.1	DOGA: crash

GINJI KUSANAGI, TAKE THIS WOMAN, MINAKO SASEBO, TO BE YOUR LAWFULLY WEDDED WIFE?

DO YOU..

I DO!

DO YOU MINAKO SASEBO, TAKE THIS... UM... GINJI KUSANAGI, TO BE YOUR LAWFULLY WEDDED HUSBAND?

I'M SORRY...

AFTER ALL...

WHAT!?

I CAN'T...

ARGGGHH!!

JUST A DREAM...

.....

WHOA!

OR AT LEAST THAT'S WHO I'M *SUPPOSED* TO BE...

I'M IN MY SECOND YEAR AT IRIE HIGH SCHOOL...

PHEW!

MY NAME IS GINJI KUSANGI...

I WAS RIDING MY MOTORCYCLE WHEN SOME GUY ATTACKED ME! I CRASHED AND WENT FLYING OFF A BRIDGE... AND SO MY SPIRIT WAS SEPARATED FROM MY PHYSICAL BODY...

SIX MONTHS AGO, I MET MINAKO SASEBO. IT WAS LOVE AT FIRST SIGHT! BUT ON THE DAY BEFORE WE WERE SUPPOSED TO GO ON OUR FIRST DATE, SOMETHING HORRIBLE HAPPENED...

BUT THEN, SOME WEIRD ANGEL TOLD ME THERE WAS A WAY TO RETURN TO MY BODY...

Weird!?

WHAT A TRAGEDY!!

THAT GUY WHO ATTACKED ME, WITH THE DREADLOCKS AND ALL THE TATTOOS--I'M STILL NOT GONNA LET HIM GET AWAY WITH WHAT HE DID TO ME! EVEN IF *AM* A PENGUIN.

IN ORDER TO GET BACK TO BEING ME, I HAD TO FIRST BE REINCARNATED AS AN ADELIE PENGUIN!!

PLEASE!! I CHANGED MY MIND! LET ME BECOME SOMETHING ELSE!! I CAN'T EVEN SWIM!!

THE PREVIOUS NIGHT...

YOU MADE YOUR DECISION, IT WAS YOUR OWN CHOICE. NOW, YOU MUST LIVE WITH IT...

C'MON! HAVE YOU EVER HEARD OF A PENGUIN THAT CAN'T SWIM!? HOW'S A GUY SUPPOSED TO GET AROUND!?

GULP!

YOU MUST PERSEVERE FOR THE WOMAN YOU LOVE...

AND REMEMBER, ALL IS FOR NAUGHT IF YOU COMMIT SUICIDE.

THE ONLY WAY YOU CAN RETURN TO YOUR PHYSICAL HUMAN BODY IS TO LIVE OUT YOUR "NATURAL" LIFE AS A PENGUIN!

HOW WOULD I KNOW?

HEY, SO WHAT'S THE AVERAGE LIFE SPAN OF AN ADELIE PENGUIN?

AND *SHE'S* THE REASON I BECAME A PENGUIN IN THE FIRST PLACE!

...MAYBE MINAKO'S FORGOTTEN ABOUT ME...

.....

SEE YA...

IT'S BEEN SIX MONTHS SINCE MY REBIRTH...

!

よいしょっ! よいしょっ!

HEY, BOSS! ARE YOU DEEP IN THOUGHT AGAIN?

THAT'S WHY I CALL YOU BOSS...

UMM...

UM...

YOU BEAT UP THE OLD BOSS AND HIS GANG, SO NOW *YOU'RE* THE BOSS!

← GINJI

BUT BOSS...

?

I THOUGHT I TOLD YOU TO QUIT CALLING ME THAT...

154

THIS IS MIKE. HE'S FAMOUS FOR BEING A GENIUS PENGUIN.

IT REALLY DOES LOOK LIKE THIS GUY'S WEARING A TUXEDO...

... I FORGOT WHAT I WAS TALKING ABOUT...

HE'S EVEN BEEN ON SOME TV COMMERCIALS.

THE TRAINERS TAUGHT ME HOW TO WRITE! IT'S FOR A NEW ROUTINE IN MY SHOW.

I WROTE IT DOWN BECAUSE I DIDN'T WANT TO FORGET!

OH! THAT'S RIGHT!!

YOU PROBABLY CAME HERE TO TELL ME SOMETHING...

HE MAY BE A GENIUS PENGUIN, BUT HE'S VERY FORGETFUL.

WAIT! WHERE'RE YOU GOING!? I REMEMBER NOW!!

I DID JUST LIKE YOU TOLD ME. I DRIPPED MY SALT EXCRETIONS* ONTO THE GUTTER DRAIN EVERYDAY.

THAT'S RIGHT!

WHAT!? THE ESCAPE TUNNEL IS COMPLETE!?

*Penguins excrete excess salt from within their bodies through ducts that pass through the nares (nostrils).

THE TIME HAS COME...

EXCELLENT!!

THE GRATE GOT RUSTY AND CAME OFF!

THE GREAT ESCAPE!!

BAAAAN

TONIGHT...

E-ESCAPE?

...

157

THREE DAYS LATER

OUCH!

NNGH

A PEN-
GUIN!?

WHAT'S
IT DOING
HERE?

.....?

WHERE AM I...?

.....

DAMN! I CAN'T REMEMBER ANYTHING AFTER THAT!

I WAS DROWNING. AND THEN...

I ESCAPED FROM THE AQUARIUM AND WENT OUT TO SEA...

SQUAAAWK!!

MEOW!

.....

.....

SOMEBODY HELP ME!!

HELP!

IT'S TRYING TO EAT ME ALIVE!!

!?

HEY! CUT THAT OUT!

COULD IT ACTUALLY BE...!?

THAT VOICE...

162

KYAAA!!

SQUAWK!

(MINAKO!)

HE'S FREAKING OUT! WHAT SHOULD I DO!?

SQUAWK! SQUAWK!!

(OH MINAKO! I'VE MISSED YOU SO MUCH!!)

SHE DOESN'T UNDERSTAND MY PENGUIN LANGUAGE...

IT'S NO USE...

SO...

HAVE YOU CALMED DOWN?

WHEN I FOUND YOU FLOATING IN THE OCEAN, I WAS AFRAID THAT YOU WERE DEAD!

.....

I'M GLAD YOU'RE FEELING BETTER!

C'MON, NOBODY'S GOING TO CARE!

WHAT AM I WAITING FOR? I SHOULD LOOK!!

AFTER ALL, I'M JUST A PENGUIN!

MINAKO COMPLETELY NAKED!!

AM I DREAMING!?

ICE WATER

YOU COULDN'T HAVE COME ALL THE WAY FROM THE SOUTH POLE, COULD YOU?

Ulp!

I JUST CAN'T FIGURE OUT WHERE YOU CAME FROM...

... NOT THAT IT MATTERS...

I'M SURE YOU'VE FORGOTTEN ALL ABOUT ME...

YOU'RE LOOKING AT THIS MISERABLE LITTLE BLACK BLOB OF A BIRD WHOSE BODY I'M TRAPPED IN...

MINAKO, I LOVE THAT INNOCENT SMILE OF YOURS... BUT I KNOW YOU'RE NOT SMILING AT ME...

...I'M JUST A PENGUIN...

...

BECAUSE NOW...

I KNOW!!

?

WHAT SHOULD I CALL YOU...?

HMM... I SHOULD THINK OF A NAME FOR YOU...

THAT'S YOUR NAME FROM NOW ON, UNDERSTAND?

"GIN-CHAN"!?

I'LL CALL YOU GIN-CHAN!! ♪

!?

DID SHE NAME *ME* AFTER *ME*!?

"GIN" AS IN "GINJI KUSANAGI"!?

YOU *HAVEN'T* FORGOTTEN ME, AFTER ALL!!!

OH, MINAKO!!

GIN-CHAN 'CAUSE YOU'RE SUCH A *CUTE LI'L PEN'GIN!!*

SHE *HAS* FORGOTTEN ABOUT ME...

It was a good feeling... while it lasted...

WHAT'S WRONG?

I TURNED INTO A PENGUIN FOR *YOU*...

AND I--

I'm so sad...

OH, MINAKO... I--

GASP!

THIS SUCKS! I *HATE* BEING A PENGUIN!

I'M DONE WASHING, GUESS I'LL GET IN THE TUB NOW...

TO BE CONTINUED IN VOL. 1

TUXEDO GIN GLOSSARY

149. BISHI: standing up straight
151.1 IRIE SUIZOKKAN PENGUIN HIROBA: Irie City Aquarium Penguins
151.2 DOKI DOKI DOKI DOKI: heart pumping
151.3 HAA HAA HAA DOKI DOKI: panting and heart pumping
152.1 DOKI DOKI: heart beat
152.2 ZAZAZA: water noise
      PUKAH: floating
152.4 KI: sharp glare
      DOOOON: melodramatic sudden appearance
152.5 JIWA: tears flowing
      U: snif
153.1 IRIE SUIZOKKAN PENGUIN HIROBA: Irie City Aquarium Penguins
153.2 OI OI OI OI: hey hey hey!
153.4 ZUKI: knife in heart type of FX
154.1 SAFAA: holy light FX
      ASERI: feeling anxious
154.2 YOISHO YOISHO: effort to move
154.4 KOO: cry of victory
155.1 GOOOOO: jet engine
155.3 PERA: flips memo book
155.4 In his notebook, Mike has written a barely legible "shio" meaning "salt."
156.1 PETA PETA PETA: webbed feet walking
156.2 GAPO: opens lid
156.3 WANA WANA WANA: Ginji trembling
156.4 GU: clenches fins
157.1 ZAPAAAN: wave hitting rocks.
157.2 ZAZAAN: waves
157.3 DON: push
157.4 DOPAAN: splash
157.5 SHIIIIN: dead silence
      ZAPAAN: wave
      BUKU BUKU: air bubbles
157.7 GUWA GUWA: penguins crying
158.2 ZAZAAAN: waves
      UUUN... UUN...: [groaning]
158.3 ZURI ZURI ZURI: body being pushed up against dock
      ZAZAZAZAZA: waves
158.4 GON: head being banged on dock
      ZAPAAAN: huge wave

159.1 BIKU: surprise
      ZAZAZAZA: wave
      UUUN: Ohhh...
159.2 UUUN ITE ITE...: ohhh... ouch ouch...
160.1 SU: suddenly wakes up
160.2 MUKU: getting up
160.3 ZUKIIN: pain in head
160.4 CHIRIN: cat bell ringing
161.1 BARI BARI BARI: scratching/chewing, being mauled
161.2 GARA: opens door
      PIKU PIKU: trembling
163.1 DON: penguin hitting her
163.2 MUGYUU: Minako prying Ginji off
163.3 HAA HAA HAA HAA ZE ZE: panting wheezing
163.4 ZUUUUN: feeling depressed
164.1 KAPOOON: water drops echoing in bathroom
164.2 CHAPOON: splash
164.3 GYU: squeeze
164.4 PUKAA: floating
165.1 NYU: looking at Gin
      DOKI: surprise
      GATA: tub shakes
165.4 ZUUUUUUN: extreme depression
165.5 UUUN: thinking
      UUU: crying
166.1 HAAU!: shock
      DAKI: hug
166.3 HA!: gasp!
166.4 UU!: surprise
167.1 ANCHOKU: "Too Easy" - meaning Minako didn't put too much thought into the name.
      SUTEEEN: slipping and falling from disappointment
167.2 PURU PURU: trembling
167.4 DARA DARA: crying eyes out
167.5 In Japan, people typically wash themselves before getting in the tub to relax and soak.
      KYU: getting up
      KURU: Ginji turning around
168.1 SHUBI: Ginji freaking out
169.1 GAAAAA: hair dryer
      BOOOOO: spaced out
169.2 CHIRIIN: cat bell
169.3 JIIIIII: glare
169.5 KURU: turning around
169.6 TOKO TOKO TOKO: walking

PART TWO:
KAGEHOSHI

NOW
DESCENDS
UPON
THEM...

HEY, OLD LADY...

WHO ARE YOU?

OH, OH YEAH!

MR. HANABISHI! SHE'S NOT OLD!!

DO YOU WANT TO WATCH THE FIREWORKS WITH US, UH, *YOUNG* LADY?

DID YOU MAKE FIRE JUST NOW, CHILD?

SHOW ME YOUR FLAME.

HEH HEH

I'D LIKE TO SEE YOU DO IT AGAIN...

WHIK

PLEASE.

!!??

?!!

174

YOU CALLED HER AN OLD LADY AGAIN, MR. HANABISHI!

CRAZY OLD LADY!

I CAN'T MAKE FLAMES!

RECCA HANABISHI...

RIGHT

REMEMBER OUR DEAL, PRINCESS.

TINK

YOU MUST HAVE SEEN THIS.

AND YOUR DEAREST DREAM SINCE CHILDHOOD IS TO BECOME A NINJA.

YOU'RE THE ELDEST SON OF SHIGEO HANABISHI, THE FIREWORKS MAKER. YOU'RE 16 YEARS OLD.

BUT YOU HAVE A SECRET ABILITY UNIQUE TO YOU!

FWAP

THERE'S NO ONE AROUND TO HEAR.

CALL FOR HELP IF YOU LIKE ...

WHAT DO YOU WANT FROM US, WITCH!!

BUT YOUR LEG, MR. HANABISHI...!!

WE DON'T KNOW WHAT SHE'S CAPABLE OF!

PRINCESS, DON'T LET HER SEE YOUR ABILITY!!

BE MINE, RECCA.

I TOLD YOU DIDN'T I? I WISH FOR DEATH. YOU MUST GIVE IT TO ME.

I DON'T KNOW YOUR PSYCHIATRIC HISTORY, BUT...

EXCUSE ME, MA'AM...

PRINCESS!!?

HELPLESS

IT'S NOT ACCEPTABLE TO PICK ON THE HELPLESS!

TA-DUM

I HAVE TO GET HIM TO THE HOSPITAL NOW!!

...

PLEASE LEAVE MR. HANABISHI ALONE! HE'S HURT!!

HUH?

LIKE YOU DID ON THE PUPPY.

WHY DON'T YOU USE YOUR HEALING POWERS, PRINCESS

UH... THEREFORE...

183

RECCA IS MINE!

YOU'RE A NUISANCE, GIRL. I WON'T HAVE YOU CONFUSING MY BOY...

WHAT'S WRONG? CAN'T YOU HEAL YOURSELF?

PRINCESS!!!

AND WE'LL BE ON OUR WAY TO THE AFTERLIFE! AND I'LL DO IT BEFORE I LET YOU HARM MY PRINCESS!

FLAME OF RECCA !!!

!!

EXPLOSIVES !!!

JUST ADD A PINCH OF...

VERY OBSERVANT.

BUT I CAN KEEP YOU FROM GETTING WHAT YOU WANT!!

I MAY NOT BE ABLE TO OUTFIGHT YOU...

HIS ONLY THOUGHT FOR THE WELFARE OF HIS MASTER!

A SHINOBI'S LIFE MEANS NOTHING!!

WHAT *ARE* YOU...!?

I'M KAGEHOSHI, MISTRESS OF SHADOWS.

FAREWELL, LOVELY RECCA...

IT WOULD BE A SHAME IF YOUR PRINCESS GOT HURT...

YOU'D BETTER BEHAVE YOURSELF NEXT TIME.

I WAS RIGHT ABOUT HER!

STOP CALLING ME MR. HANABISHI!! CALL ME RECCA!

JUST DO ME ONE FAVOR.

IT WOULD BE A SHAME IF YOUR PRINCESS GOT HURT...

YOU'D BETTER BEHAVE YOURSELF NEXT TIME.

NO MATTER WHO COMES AFTER HER..

FOR HER, I'M WILLING TO GIVE UP MY LIFE.

SHE SHIELDED ME WITH HER OWN BODY...

NOW I REALLY AM A SHINOBI,

READY TO RISK MY LIFE FOR MY MASTER.

NO "MR."-- JUST "RECCA"!!

MR. RECCA!!

...THE DOOR OF DESTINY OPENED.

AND...

AND SO RECCA HANABISHI AND YANAGI SAKOSHITA MET.

TO BE CONTINUED IN VOL. I

**editor's
choice**

ed•i•tor's choice (ed'i-tôrs chois) *n.* **1.** That which defines cutting-edge.
2. Manga known for its daring, creativity, and artistry. **3.** Ground-breaking
stories that change the way manga is read. **4.** Manga that sets the
standard for excellence and reveals its promise.

Editor's Choice titles from **VIZ***:*

Cinderalla • Collector File • Dance Till Tomorrow • Flowers and Bees • Gyo • Hansel &
Gretel • Maison Ikkoku • No. 5 • Phoenix • Princess Mermaid • Short Cuts • Vagabond

DO YOU FEEL BETTER, KAORI?

NO...I'M STILL NOT GREAT...

BZZZZ

WELL, THIS IS THE FISH MARKET.

GOD, IT STINKS...

YOU SHOULD TAKE A SHOWER, TOO.

UM-HM.

ARE YOU BETTER NOW?

HUH?

NO WAY! NOT UNTIL YOU BRUSH YOUR TEETH.

I DON'T WANT TO SMELL YOUR BAD BREATH.

HOW ABOUT A KISS FIRST?

YES I DID. I JUST PUT UP WITH IT EVER SINCE WE STARTED GOING OUT.

BUT YOU DIDN'T MIND KISSING ME BEFORE.

HAAH

JUST A LITTLE...

I HAVE BAD BREATH?

BUT I DO BRUSH MY TEETH... TWICE A DAY...

SO BRUSH YOUR TEETH FROM NOW ON, OKAY?

BUT I CAN'T TAKE IT ANY-MORE.

YOU JUST--

THAT WOULD BE NICE.

IF WE KISS TEN TIMES A DAY THEN I HAVE TO BRUSH TEN TIMES?

ARE YOU SAYING I HAVE TO DO IT EVERY TIME WE KISS?

GIVE ME A BREAK! I CAN'T DEAL WITH YOUR NEUROSES!!

198

I'M GOING BACK TO TOKYO! I'M LEAVING TONIGHT!

FINE! YOU DON'T HAVE TO BE SUCH AN ASSHOLE!

WILL YOU LISTEN TO YOURSELF?

IF YOU DON'T WANT TO BE HERE, WHY DON'T YOU JUST LEAVE?

SLAM

THEN DO IT!

IT'S GETTING DARK. YOU'RE NOT REALLY GOING TO FLY BACK TO TOKYO!

THERE'S SNAKES OUT THERE!!

HEY, KAORI! WHAT ABOUT YOUR THINGS?!

SHAAAA

DAMN IT...

...

KAORI! WHERE ARE YOU?

KAORI!

WHAT WAS THAT?

WHAT'S THAT SMELL?

HM?

200

AIEEEE!

AH?

WOW... IT REALLY REEKS...

WHAT'S WRONG, KAORI?

THERE YOU ARE.

I WAS LOOKING ALL OVER TOWN FOR YOU.

SHFFFFF

WHAT? IS IT A SNAKE?

TADASHI...THERE'S SOMETHING IN THE GRASS...

AAGGH!

SHHHHHHHHWHHHHH

HUH !?

WHAT IS THIS *SMELL* !?

GET ME OUT OF HERE!

IT'S NOT A SNAKE... A CAT MAYBE?

WHAT WAS THAT!?

WSHWSHWSH WSH

COME ON... LET'S GO BACK TO THE ROOM...

NO KIDDING. IT'S SOMETHING PUTRID... ROTTEN GARBAGE...

202

FSSHHH

IT ISN'T GOING AWAY.

I CAN STILL SMELL IT!

...

...

TADASHI!

IN FACT... IT'S NOT JUST STICKING TO US...

I KNOW.

TADASHI! DO SOMETHING!!

IT'S INSIDE THE HOUSE...

IT SMELLS HERE, TOO...

...WHILE YOU GO AND BUY AIR FRESHENER! ALL RIGHT?

OKAY? I'M GOING TO TAKE ANOTHER SHOWER...

THERE'S NOTHING I CAN DO ABOUT THIS SMELL...

...GIVE ME A BREAK.

GO BUY SOME DIS-INFECTANT! SOME AIR FRESHENER! ANYTHING!

204

SNIFF...

...

DID THE WIND BLOW IT AWAY?

THAT'S FUNNY... IT DOESN'T SMELL OUTSIDE...

IT'S GETTING STRONGER !!

ARGH!

WHAT IS GOING ON!?

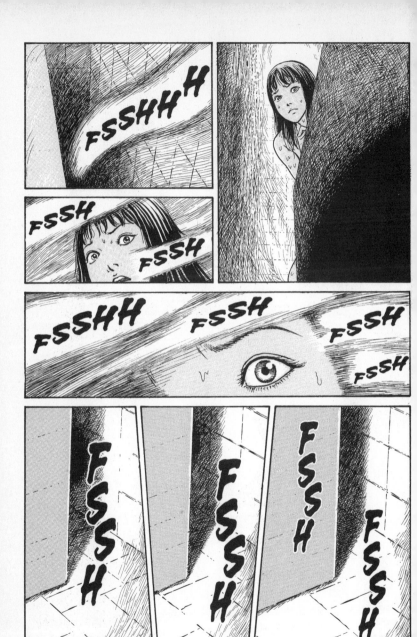

EEEYAAHH!

CLIK

208

209

WHAT IS THIS SOUND?

BUMP

FSSSSSSSHHHHHHHH

FSSSSSSSHHHHHHHH

FSSSSHHHHH

K TOK TOK TOK

!

FSSSSSSSSHHHH

BUMP

!

WH-WHAT WAS THAT?

COULDN'T HAVE BEEN A CAT...

TOK TOK TOK TOK TOK

TOK

CLIK

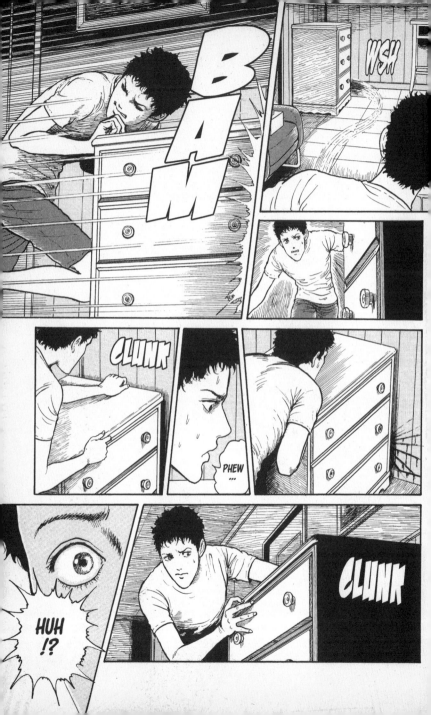

TO BE CONTINUED IN VOL. 1

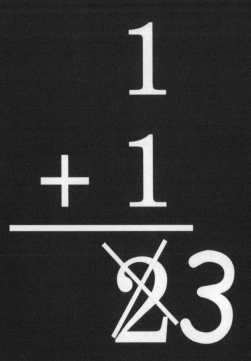

Buy any TWO VIZ manga titles get ONE FREE*.

Vagabond

By Takehiko Inoue

"...a must for fans."
-Scott Green, Ain't It Cool News

"If you're a fan of Japanese history, you need this...It's that good."
-Patrick King, Animefringe

"Some of the most beautiful pen-and-ink work in any comic being published now."
-Adi Tantimedh, ArtBomb

"With often breathtaking art, this makes for an extremely satisfying comics experience."
-Tony Isabella, Comics Buyer's Guide

"Viz is giving readers a lot of bang for their comic buck with this one."
-Dani Fletcher, Sequential Tart

AWARDS

2000 Kodansha Award for Best Manga

2002 Tezuka Award for Best Manga

2000 Media Arts Award from the Japanese Ministry of Culture

Over 22 million copies sold worldwide!

InuYasha™

Rated #1 on Cartoon Network's Adult Swim!

In its original unedited form.

maison ikkoku™

The beloved romantic comedy of errors—a fan favorite!

Available on DVD in Summer 2003!

Ranma ½™

The zany, wacky study of martial arts at its best!

Anime-zing OFFER!

$3 Off*

*(regular price)

Any VIZ Anime DVD!

Offer not valid with any other sale price or promotional offer.
See SUNCOAST sales associate for details. Offer expires 10/31/03.

SUNCOAST™

The store for movie lovers.

COMPLETE OUR SURVEY AND LET US KNOW WHAT YOU THINK!

☐ Please check here if you DO NOT wish to receive information or future offers from VIZ

Name: _____

Address: _____

City: _____ State: _____ Zip: _____

E-mail: _____

☐ Male ☐ Female Date of Birth (mm/dd/yyyy): ___/___/___ (Under 13? Parental consent required)

What race/ethnicity do you consider yourself? (please check one)

☐ Asian/Pacific Islander   ☐ Black/African American   ☐ Hispanic/Latino

☐ Native American/Alaskan Native ☐ White/Caucasian   ☐ Other: _____

What VIZ product did you purchase? (check all that apply and indicate title purchased)

☐ DVD/VHS _____

☐ Graphic Novel _____

☐ Magazines _____

☐ Merchandise _____

Reason for purchase: (check all that apply)

☐ Special offer   ☐ Favorite title   ☐ Gift

☐ Recommendation   ☐ Other _____

Where did you make your purchase? (please check one)

☐ Comic store   ☐ Bookstore   ☐ Mass/Grocery Store

☐ Newsstand   ☐ Video/Video Game Store ☐ Other: _____

☐ Online (site: _____)

What other VIZ properties have you purchased/own? _____

_____

How many anime and/or manga titles have you purchased in the last year? How many were VIZ titles? (please check one from each column)

ANIME

☐ None
☐ 1-4
☐ 5-10
☐ 11+

MANGA

☐ None
☐ 1-4
☐ 5-10
☐ 11+

VIZ

☐ None
☐ 1-4
☐ 5-10
☐ 11+

I find the pricing of VIZ products to be: (please check one)

☐ Cheap   ☐ Reasonable   ☐ Expensive

What genre of manga and anime would you like to see from VIZ? (please check two)

☐ Adventure   ☐ Comic Strip   ☐ Detective   ☐ Fighting
☐ Horror   ☐ Romance   ☐ Sci-Fi/Fantasy   ☐ Sports

What do you think of VIZ's new look?

☐ Love It   ☐ It's OK   ☐ Hate It   ☐ Didn't Notice   ☐ No Opinion

THANK YOU! Please send the completed form to:

NJW Research
42 Catharine St.
Poughkeepsie, NY 12601